MOLLUSCS

by
Madeline Tyler

BookLife
PUBLISHING

©2018
BookLife Publishing
King's Lynn
Norfolk PE30 4LS

A catalogue record for this
book is available from the
British Library.

ISBN: 978-1-78637-350-2

Written by:
Madeline Tyler

Edited by:
John Wood

Designed by:
Danielle Jones

All facts, statistics, web addresses and URLs in this book were verified as valid and accurate at time of writing.
No responsibility for any changes to external websites or references can be accepted by either the author or publisher.

PHOTOCREDITS

CONTENTS

Words that look like <u>this</u> are explained in the glossary on page 31.

THE ANIMAL KINGDOM

The animal kingdom includes over eight million known living <u>species</u>. They come in many different shapes and sizes, they each do weird and wonderful things and they live all over planet Earth.

From the freezing Arctic waters to the hottest desert in the world, animals have <u>adapted</u> to the often extreme and diverse conditions on Earth.

Even though each and every species of animal is <u>unique</u>, they still share certain characteristics with each other. These shared characteristics are used to classify animals. There are six main groups used to classify animals. They are; mammals, reptiles, birds, insects, amphibians and fish.

10,000 new species of animal are discovered **every year.**

Some smaller animal classification groups include molluscs and marsupials. Molluscs include snails, slugs, cuttlefish, octopuses and squid.

WHAT IS A MOLLUSC?

A mollusc is a type of animal that has a soft body, a <u>mantle</u> and a special tongue called a radula. Some molluscs also have a hard shell.

Some molluscs, like squid, are aquatic, which means that they must live in water in order to survive. Other molluscs, like some slugs and snails, live on land. Molluscs are cold-blooded which means that their body temperature changes with the temperature of the environment. Land molluscs keep warm by laying out in the sun.

Squid spend most of their time on their own, but when they come together in a group they are called a shoal of squid.

There are between 50,000 and 100,000 species of molluscs alive today. Although molluscs share some characteristics, each species has adapted differently to allow it to survive in its habitat. Mussels, oysters, octopuses, slugs and snails are all types of mollusc.

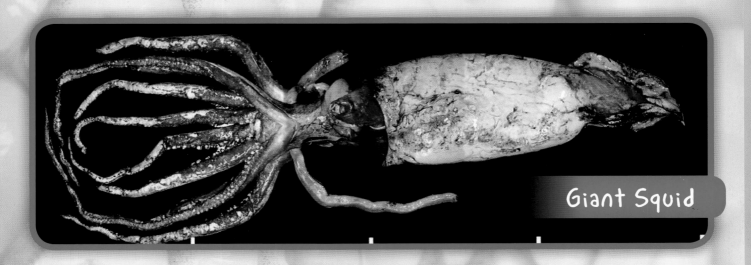

Giant Squid

The giant squid is one of the largest molluscs in the world. The largest giant squid ever recorded was 13 metres (m) long, but some people believe that they can grow even bigger! Acmella nana is one of the smallest molluscs. They are the smallest snails in the world and are only 0.7 millimetres (mm).

Acmella Nana

MOLLUSC CHECKLIST

- Soft body
- Radula
- Invertebrate
- Cold-blooded
- Mantle (or shell)
- Lays eggs

BODY PARTS

There are lots of different molluscs and they all look very different. However, they do have some things in common that mean they can be grouped together.

All molluscs are invertebrates, which means that they do not have skeletons. Their bodies are soft and squishy. Each type of mollusc has tentacles or a foot which they use to move around. Many molluscs also have a radula inside their mouths. This is like a tongue with teeth and it is used to chew food.

Shell

Radula

Foot

Squishy Body

SHELLS

Most types of molluscs have shells that grow from their mantles. Snails, clams, limpets and mussels all have hard shells that protect them from danger. As molluscs grow bigger, so do their shells. Some shells are able to repair themselves if there are any small cracks. Mussels and clams are usually completely covered by their shell and only open up to feed, breathe and <u>reproduce</u>. However, some molluscs, like octopuses and slugs, do not have a shell.

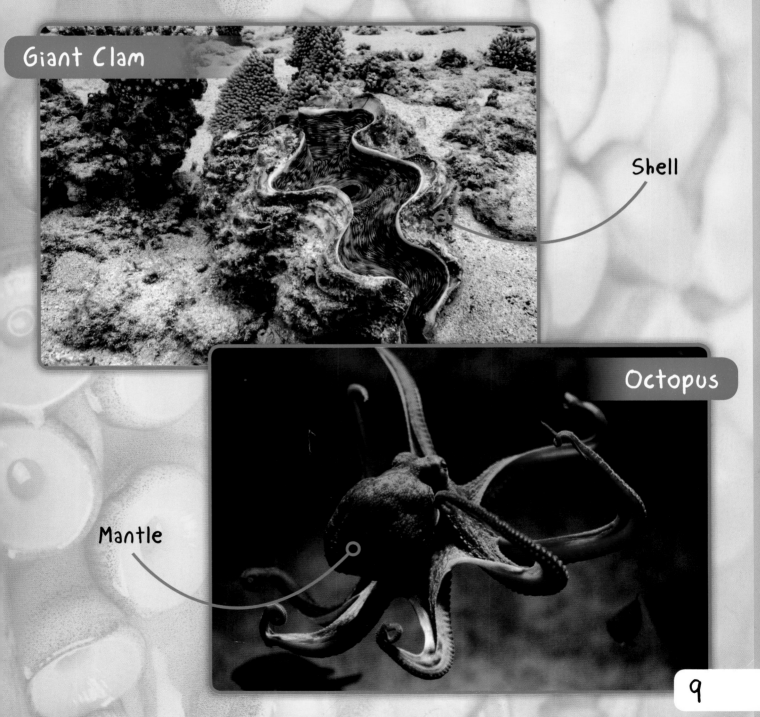

Giant Clam

Shell

Octopus

Mantle

TENTACLES

Many molluscs, like octopuses, squid and cuttlefish, have tentacles. These tentacles usually have suction cups or little hooks that help the animals to catch their prey or to protect them from danger. Tentacles are also useful to help a mollusc move around.

The majority of an octopus's <u>neurons</u> are found in its tentacles. This means that octopus tentacles can move without being controlled by the brain.

To test this, some scientists cut off an octopus's tentacle from its body. The tentacle still reacted to being touched and tickled!

If an **octopus** loses a **tentacle**, they can **grow** a new one.

Tentacl

Suction Cups (Suckers)

Slugs and snails also have tentacles, but they are very different to octopus or squid tentacles. They are much shorter and do not have suckers on. Slugs and snails use their tentacles to see and smell the world around them.

The longer ones at the top have eyes at the end and are called eye-stalks. The shorter ones let the mollusc smell its environment. They help it to know where food can be found.

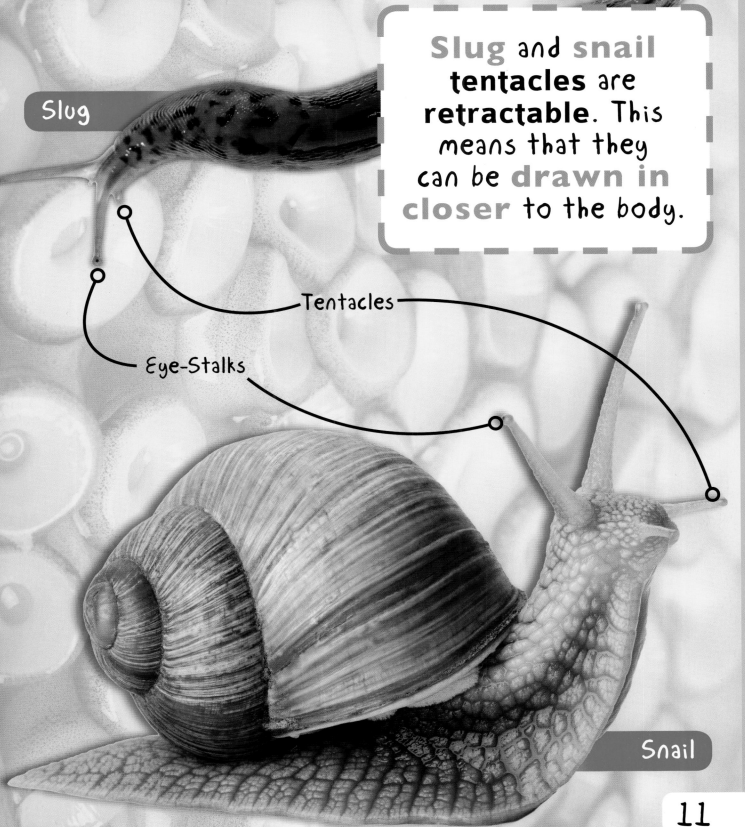

Slug

Slug and **snail** **tentacles** are **retractable**. This means that they can be **drawn in closer** to the body.

Tentacles

Eye-Stalks

Snail

11

GETTING AROUND

Most land molluscs get around by using their foot to crawl across the ground. The bottom of the foot is very flat and smooth. The muscles in the foot contract (get smaller) and relax (get bigger) to wrinkle up the foot. This creates a rippling movement that pushes the slug or snail forward, slowly but steadily.

Keep an eye out for snail and slug slime where you live.

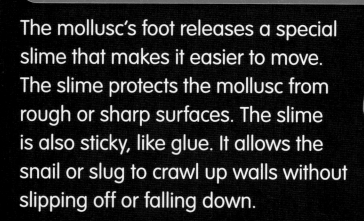

The mollusc's foot releases a special slime that makes it easier to move. The slime protects the mollusc from rough or sharp surfaces. The slime is also sticky, like glue. It allows the snail or slug to crawl up walls without slipping off or falling down.

BREATHING

Some molluscs live in water while others live on land. Just like fish, aquatic molluscs have gills that allow them to breathe underwater. In octopuses and squid, the gills are inside the mantle cavity (a space underneath the mantle). They fill the mantle cavity with water to get <u>oxygen</u> into the gills and the bloodstream.

Fish Gills

If octopuses and squid force water out of their mantle cavity quick enough, they can move themselves forward. This is called jet propulsion.

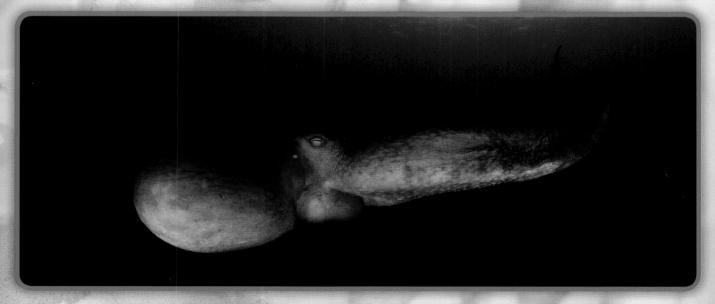

Land molluscs breathe using the mantle cavity too. Most have <u>permeable</u> skin over their bodies which lets oxygen through and a simple lung in their mantle cavity.

PREDATORS
AND PREY

All animals can be sorted into groups depending on what they eat. The three groups are carnivores, herbivores and omnivores.

Molluscs can be either herbivores, omnivores or carnivores and it can sometimes depend on what food is available. Octopuses are usually carnivores. They hunt and eat animals like crabs, snails, shrimp and small fish. However, if there is not a lot of food available, they can also eat underwater plants.

Herbivores
Plant-eaters

Carnivores
Meat-eaters

Omnivores
Plant and meat-eaters

Mussels

Whelk

Land slugs and snails are mostly herbivores. They eat leafy plants and rotting plant matter. Whelks, a type of sea snail, are carnivores. They eat worms and other molluscs, like clams, oysters and mussels. Clams, oysters and mussels are filter feeders. They filter the water and get <u>nutrients</u> from very small creatures like plankton.

Animals that hunt other animals are called predators, whereas animals that are hunted are called prey.

Some species of molluscs are predators, while others are the prey. Large molluscs like the giant Pacific octopus are deadly predators. They are some of the biggest creatures in the sea and use their tentacles to catch their prey. They eat small sharks but are preyed on by great white sharks.

Birds, mice and toads all eat snails. They are a common prey because they are small and very slow. Snails try to protect themselves by retreating into their shell or by producing slime that doesn't taste very nice to the predator.

A snail kite has caught this snail.

15

FRESHWATER

Habitats are the homes of plants and animals. They provide food and shelter that allow the living things to survive. Molluscs can be found in lots of different habitats including on the land and in water. Some molluscs, like snails, can be found on land, in the sea and in freshwater.

Sea Snail

Cuttlefish belong to the same <u>class</u> as octopuses and squid. They look quite similar and have long tentacles with suckers along them. Cuttlefish usually liv in shallow waters and eat crabs, shrimp, fish and sometimes even octopuse.

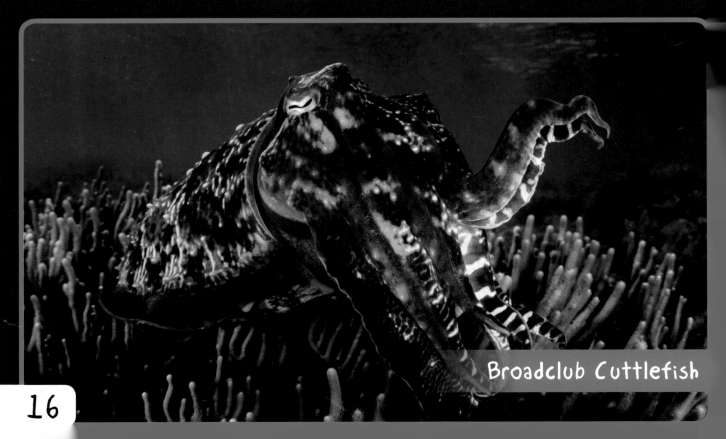
Broadclub Cuttlefish

Apple snails are freshwater molluscs. They are a type of snail that comes from South America and Africa but can now be found across the world. Apple snails have gills that allow them to take oxygen from the water. They live in ponds, swamps and rivers and spend most of their time underwater to hide from their main predators: birds.

Apple Snail

Garden snails are sometimes called **European brown garden snails.**

Garden snails are very common land snails. They can be found all over the world and like to live in places where there are lots of leafy plants, like gardens. Garden snails are often considered a pest because they eat plants and crops.

17

ADAPTATION

Molluscs have adapted to their environments in many amazing ways.

An adaptation is a way that a plant or animal changes over a long time to help it survive in its environment. The Californian sea hare uses camouflage to blend in with its surroundings to hide from predators. It changes colour depending on what colour seaweed or algae it eats. This helps it to hide whilst it is feeding.

If they are **attacked**, **sea hares** can produce a cloud of **colourful** ink to **distract** the **predator**.

Californian Sea Hare

Apple snails are amphibious. This means that they can breathe on land and underwater. Apple snails have adapted to have both a lung and a gill. If there is not a lot of oxygen in the water, or if the water dries up in a <u>drought</u>, the snails can come onto land.

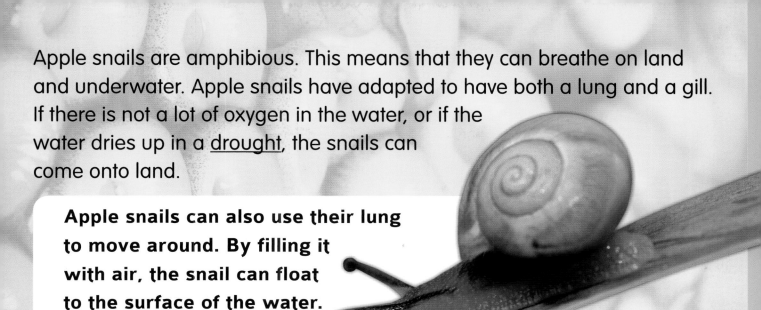

Apple snails can also use their lung to move around. By filling it with air, the snail can float to the surface of the water. The shell doesn't weigh them down so they can move more easily.

Female apple snails lay their eggs above water so that fish cannot eat them.

LIFE CYCLES

The life cycle of an animal is the series of changes that it goes through from the start to the end of its life.

Life cycles of molluscs are all unique. However, there are some similarities between them. For example, all molluscs lay eggs. The eggs have to be <u>fertilised</u> before they can hatch. Most molluscs need a male to fertilise their eggs, but some species of snail can fertilise their own eggs. This is called self-fertilisation.

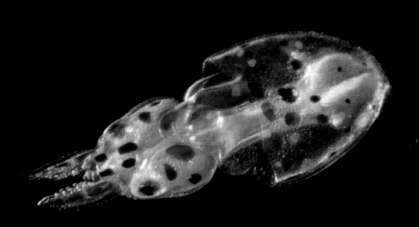

Squid Larvae

When **octopus** and **squid** eggs **hatch**, the young are called **larvae**.

LIFE CYCLE OF A MUSSEL

The life cycle of a **mussel** is similar to the life cycle of a **clam**. Mussels and clams are very similar — they are both **shelled** molluscs that live in the **water**.

Freshwater mussels carry their eggs in pouches called gills.

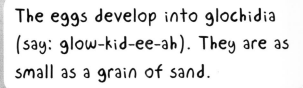

The eggs develop into glochidia (say: glow-kid-ee-ah). They are as small as a grain of sand.

The female mussels release the glochidia into the water. The glochidia must find a host fish that they can attach to.

The glochidia form a <u>cyst</u> on the fish and stay there for several weeks. Eventually, they change into small mussels and fall off the fish to the bottom of the water.

LIFE CYCLE OF A SNAIL

Most species of snails are <u>hermaphrodites</u>. This means that they are neither male or female, so any snail can produce a set of eggs. They lay their eggs in a nest hole in the soil.

After around four weeks, the snail larvae hatch out of the eggs.

The larvae have a shell but must eat lots of <u>calcium</u> for the shell to grow hard and strong.

Snails continue to grow for around two years, until they become adults and are ready to produce their own eggs.

LIFE CYCLE OF AN OCTOPUS

The male octopus uses one of his tentacles to put his <u>sperm</u> inside the female octopus's mantle cavity. A few months after this, the male will die.

A female octopus lays between 50 and 100 eggs, but some can lay up to 100,000 eggs. She carries them in a space between her tentacles for several months.

The female octopus guards her eggs very carefully and, during this time, she doesn't eat anything. After the eggs hatch into larvae, the female octopus dies from <u>exhaustion</u>.

Octopus larvae feed on plankton and become adults after around two years.

EXTREME MOLLUSCS

GIANT SQUID

Some molluscs have developed extreme habits, skills or features that help them to survive.

The giant squid is one of the largest species of squid in the world. These squids usually grow to around 10 metres long. The largest giant squid ever measured was 13 metres long, although some scientists think others could grow to be around 18 metres long. Giant squid live very deep down in the ocean and have developed a very useful characteristic that helps them to see when there is very little sunlight. Giant squid have very large eyes that allow them to spot prey and also any predators that may want to eat them.

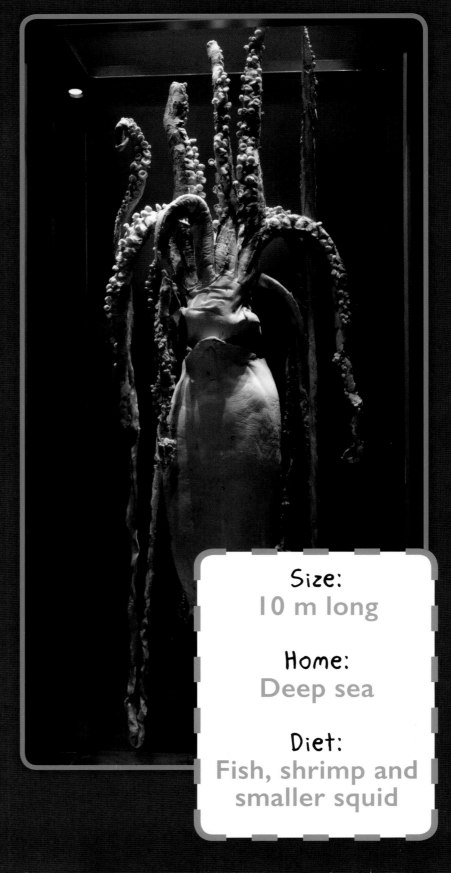

Size:
10 m long

Home:
Deep sea

Diet:
Fish, shrimp and smaller squid

GIANT AFRICAN LAND SNAIL

The giant African land snail is a very large land snail. Giant African land snails are nocturnal. This means that they are awake and active during the night but sleep underground during the day. By burying themselves in the soil, the snails can stay cool and hide from predators.

If it is very hot or very cold, giant African land snails go into hibernation. They become very slow and spend a lot of time sleeping. This is so that they can use their energy to either heat up or cool down.

Size:
20 centimetres (cm) long

Home:
Coastlands, forests and shrublands in East Africa

Diet:
Plant material, fruit and vegetables

VIOLET SEA SNAIL

The violet sea snail is also called the bubble raft snail because of an amazing skill that the snail has. Bubble raft snails produce a <u>mucus</u> that they mix with air using their foot to make bubbles.

The snails use the bubbles like a raft to float on top of the water. They drift through the water for the rest of their lives and catch any food that floats past them.

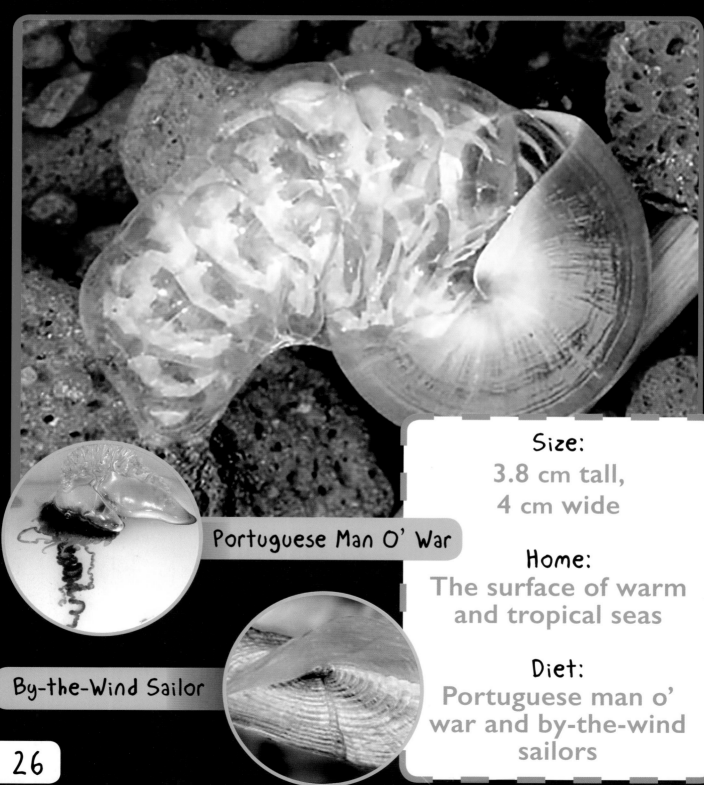

Portuguese Man O' War

By-the-Wind Sailor

Size:
3.8 cm tall,
4 cm wide

Home:
The surface of warm
and tropical seas

Diet:
Portuguese man o'
war and by-the-wind
sailors

PINCTADA OYSTERS

Pinctada oysters are a type of oyster that produce shiny gems called pearls. Although their shells may look very ordinary on the outside, their inner shell is made of nacre. Nacre is shiny and is sometimes called mother of pearl. This is because it is the same material that oysters layer up to produce pearls. Pearls are made when something very small, like a grain of sand, enters the oyster's shell. The oyster covers the bit of sand with lots of layers of nacre so that its insides do not get <u>irritated</u>. After many, many layers, a pearl is made!

Pearls are very pretty and are often used to make jewellery.

Size: 7 cm to 35 cm long
Home: Indian Ocean and Pacific Ocean
Diet: Small plankton or algae

MOLLUSCS UNDER THREAT

Many species of mollusc are in danger of becoming <u>extinct</u>. Lots of the molluscs in this book live in our oceans. Humans are <u>polluting</u> the oceans with rubbish and waste that can harm underwater habitats and kill sea life.

Although plastic is very useful and is used to make lots of things, sea creatures can get very ill if they eat it. It is important to always recycle plastic so that the oceans stay clean and the sea creatures stay healthy.

Some people have a special bin so that they can recycle their rubbish. Do you have one?

Freshwater mollusc habitats are also being polluted and damaged. One major problem that freshwater molluscs face is deforestation. This is when humans cut down forests in order to collect the wood and use the land for farming. As the forests disappear, there are fewer roots to hold all the soil in place. The rainwater washes all the loose soil into the rivers and lakes which damages the habitats and can even kill the wildlife living there.

Deforestation also destroys the habitats of land molluscs like snails and slugs.

FIND OUT MORE

GO EXPLORING

Would you like to find out more about different species of mollusc? Or maybe even see some for yourself? Try looking in your garden, walking along the beach or visiting an <u>aquarium</u> to see what creatures you can discover.

WEBSITES

GO WILD
www.gowild.wwf.org.uk

On this website you can follow links to information on all sorts of endangered animals and find out what WWF is doing to save wildlife.

BBC NATURE
www.bbc.co.uk/nature/life/ Mollusca

Learn about different species of mollusc and their habitats.

GLOSSARY

adapted	changed over time to suit the environment
aquarium	a place containing tanks of many different sea creatures
calcium	a mineral used to grow strong bones and teeth in humans and hard shells in some molluscs
class	a large group of living things that share important characteristics (e.g. mammals)
cyst	a small pouch on the body that contains liquid or air
drought	a long period of very little rainfall, which leads to a lack of water
exhaustion	to be very tired and have little energy
extinct	when a species of animal is no longer alive
fertilised	causing an egg to develop into a new living thing
hermaphrodites	living organisms that have male and female organs
invertebrate	an animal that does not have a backbone
irritated	to be sore
mantle	the body walls which cover or contain the organs and digestive system of a mollusc
mucus	a slimy substance
neurons	nerve cells
nutrients	natural substances that plants and animals need to grow and stay healthy
oxygen	a natural gas that all living things need in order to survive
permeable	something that allows liquid or gas to pass through it
polluting	making poisonous or dirty by the actions of humans
reproduce	to produce young through the act of mating
species	a group of very similar animals or plants that are capable of producing young together
sperm	a cell found in male animals that carries the information necessary to create new life
unique	being the only one of its kind

INDEX